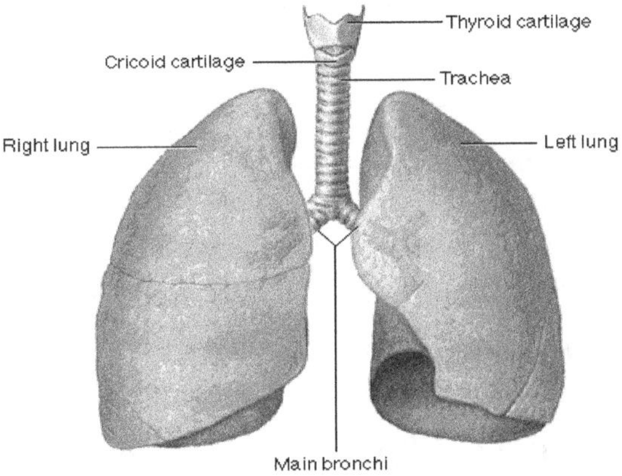

HOW TO QUIT SMOKING FOREVER

BY SUSAN SEYMOUR

Dip. Hypnotherapy, MICHP

TABLE OF CONTENTS

INTRODUCTION

You are reading this because you want to give up smoking and need help

The purpose of this book is to help you to stop smoking forever. It deals with urges to smoke again and gives helpful tips. In just one week you can be smoke free is you want to be.

WHAT YOU NEED TO KNOW

1. YOU NEED TO KNOW HOW TO FIGHT THE URGES TO SMOKE
2. YOU NEED TO KNOW THE REASONS YOU WANT TO INHALE SMOKE

3. YOU NEED TO ASK YOURSELF IF YOU ARE READY TO QUIT
4. YOU NEED TO KNOW THAT YOU CAN DO IT SUCCESSFULLY
5. WHAT DO YOU NEED TO DETERMINE YOUR SUCCESS?
   A. YOU MUST HAVE DESIRE TO GIVE UP THE BAD HABIT
   B. YOU MUST HAVE KNOWLEDGE AND CONFIDENCE THAT YOU CAN DO IT
   C. YOU NEED MOTIVATION

First you need to be motivated and energised to quit.

Secondly you need a plan of how you intend to do it

Thirdly you need a start date for quitting

Fourthly you need emotional support from a friend or loved one

Fifth you need to remove yourself from temptation.

It is possible for everyone to be motivated to quit smoking. However some temptations or stresses can cause the process to fail. Many people give up, often for years, and go back to smoking when they have a stress trigger.

Quitting smoking can be a very uncomfortable experience and the changes to our body and minds as we reduce the nicotine drug can often make us give in. Many who finally manage to give up have tried lots of times in the past. It is important to not have any doubts in your ability to give up. If you have then perhaps you should consider that you are not ready.

This book is intended to give you all the information you need to help you to give up FOREVER.

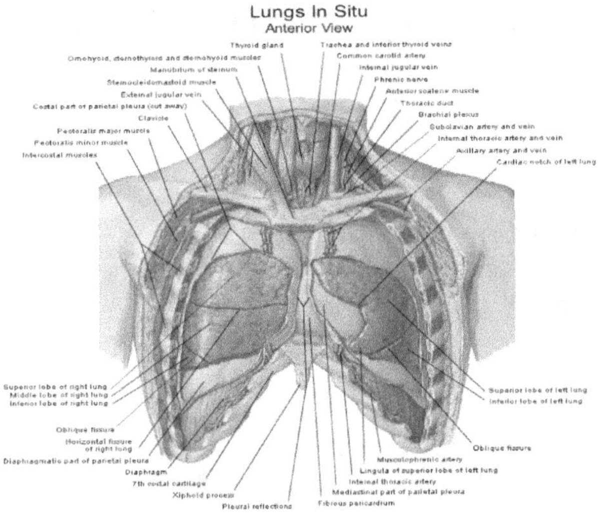

Look at the thyroid gland at the top of the lungs. The heat from the cigarettes burns the thyroid cells/ These in turn regulate the metabolism of the body. The thyroid also regulates the aging process.

Smoking cannabis affects the thyroid even more as it burns at a higher temperature.

PREPARATION IS THE KEY TO SUCCESS

You will need:

1. Charts
2. Nicotine chewing gum (30)
3. **A DAILY PROTOCOL:**

Morning

1 x 200mcg chromium to balance blood sugar

1 x chewable 1,000 Vitamin C to balance adrenals

1 x vitamin B complex to reduce stress levels

Evening

Repeat all the above

During the day

Take one drop of energetic homeopathic when you get a cigarette craving

If required buy Nicotine lozenges or chewing gum. Do not use patches they can often increase your desire to smoke

THE RISKS OF SMOKING

According to health care experts, if you smoke, you will be twelve times more likely to die from lung cancer. It's very important for you to increase your chances of living from two to twelve times longer, gain many extra years of happy, healthy existence, and save money?

- 10 times more likely to die from Cancers of the mouth, throat, and oesophagus risks.
- 12 times more likely to die from lung cancer or some form of lung diseases.
- 10 times more likely to die from cancer of the larynx.
- 6 times more likely to die of heart disease.
- You will be twice as likely to die of a stroke.

Lungs

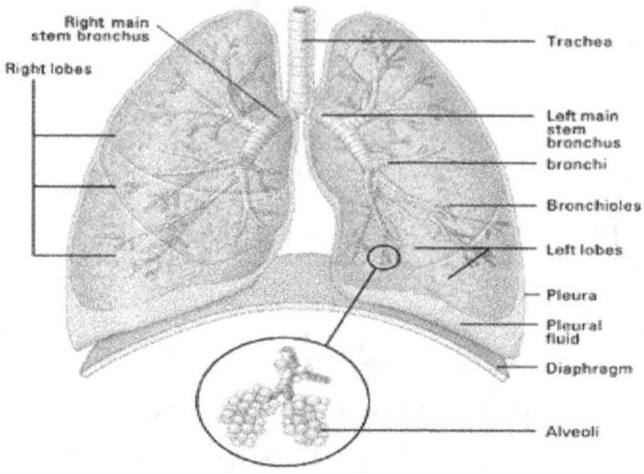

The alveoli are grape-like formations that filter the CO2 and Oxygen. When people smoke these little round filters "pop" and join together to form one large round filter, then these too "pop" under stress to form even larger filters. Each time reducing the effectiveness of the oxygen transfer needed for the heart. In addition the tiny filter hairs in the trachea lie flat causing the removal of mucous to be limited. Often a reason for "smokers cough". The tar from each cigarette collects in the lungs turning them from a healthy pink to a beige, half dead colour.

MONEY IN THE BANK

Another overlooked benefit is the amount of money saved by not buying cigarettes in the first place. For example if you smoke one pack of cigarettes a day at 5.00 per pack, you spend 1,825 per year. If your habit has continued for a period of 10 years you will have spent an incredible 18,250! If you smoke two packs for that same period of time, you will spend 36,500!
If you want to help yourself to be successful, you need to be able to answer the following two questions:

1) What can you do to reduce the desire to smoke every time the craving hits you?
2) What will you do until the urge passes?

With the information contained in this book, you will be given the ammunition you need in this war against tobacco. You will be able to resist the urge to smoke every time you get the craving and you should be able to resist it until the urge passes. Next, you will need to deal with the reasons of why you smoke now. What kind of satisfaction does smoking give you - physical, mental, or emotional? Ask yourself these questions and write down the answers.

KNOW YOUR ENEMY

Nicotine creates a biochemical reaction in your body that has an immediate effect on your mood, your ability to reason, and your metabolism. Even if you only smoke a few cigarettes a day, you do feel bad when you try to quit? The more that you smoke, the higher level of chemical dependency will be reached. Light smokers can also become just as dependent on cigarettes because of nicotine's psychological impact. In this way it can affect moods and feelings in certain situations.

It is only a matter of seconds after that first puff that nicotine starts to have an effect on your central nervous system, and the rest of your body. Certain areas of the brain, when stimulated by nicotine, help you think more clearly. Other areas of the brain lie in a pleasure centre which when stimulated can make you feel more relaxed and less anxious.

Nicotine also affects the hormones produced by the body, which creates a chemical dependency to nicotine and the accompanying craving. Heavy smokers have become denendent on the heightened levels of hormones, stimulated by nicotine, which can have an addictive quality. They need a cigarette at certain intervals of time. After the stimulation of the hormones starts to fall, they need another cigarette to bring them back into the comfort zone. If they do not get that cigarette, the craving begins. The adrenal glands are greatly affected. This lack of stimulation can be the cause of headaches while withdrawing.

HOW YOU CAN EASILY QUIT SMOKING

Quitting is hard. If you have tried to quit smoking, you know how hard it can be. It is hard because nicotine is a very addictive drug some times it can be as addictive as heroin or cocaine.

Many people have found that including physical activity in their program to quit smoking has added a tremendous benefit to assist in quitting. There are many reasons for this:
When people are more active, they gain confidence and like themselves more. They feel more energy, and are more capable of dealing with tension in their lives. With increased activity, the smell of tobacco actually becomes offensive. Whenever you feel the need to smoke after you have decided to quit, get up, and move around instead. A brief physical activity can provide you with the lift that you may have received from nicotine.

It usually takes around two weeks for the mind and body to adjust to not having any cravings. Much like any detox you need to be patient. Doing it slowly and gradually works best. For more help buy a good hypnotherapy CD and listen daily.

QUIT SMOKING IN A WEEK

Look at the following Reasons for Quitting: -

- You will live longer and live better.
- Become a high-energy person without cigarettes.
- Quitting will lower your chance of having a heart attack
- Reduce the chance of Cancers of the lung, mouth and throat
- Relax and enjoy the pleasure of relaxation without cigarettes.
- Deal with your tensions without a cigarette.
- If you are pregnant women, this will improve chances of having a healthy baby.
- The people you live with, especially family members will be healthier.
- Save money.

Consider the following question: - How and when do you want to quit smoking?

There are only two ways to effectively quit smoking, immediately (cold turkey), or gradually. When you quit gradually, you use various methods to taper off before you have that last cigarette. Neither way is better than the other for all people. Pick the one that you feel fits your temperament. Either way, nicotine gum may prove to be a real benefit in giving up, especially if you are a heavy smoker.
Try this test to see which way is better for you.

CHOOSE THE RIGHT METHOD OF QUITING FOR YOU – the quiz

Answer the questions by circling "yes", "no", or "not sure".

1. Stopping smoking is one of the most important things in the world for me right now.
   Yes [ ]   no   [ ]   not sure   [ ]

2. I can handle a tough problem without a smoke.

Yes [ ] no [ ] not sure [ ]

4. I have to quit smoking and my reasons are good enough to do it now.

Yes [ ] no [ ] not sure [ ]

5. If I quit this minute, I know I can find a way to resist the craving to smoke, even if it is strong.
Yes [ ] no [ ] not sure [ ]

If your answer to all of the above questions is 'yes', you may be a candidate to quit immediately. But before you do, read on to get the tools necessary to be successful. After reading the following, set a time to quit. If not right now, then set a date, but <u>do it.</u>

What about the doubts you may be feeling now?

Most smokers will get a sense of doubt when they read the questions above. You probably are not confident in your ability to follow through with resisting any future craving to smoke, or finding something to substitute for the feelings that smoking has given to you.

In order to have the confidence to quit you:

(1) Must find an alternative to handle the urge to smoke, when it hits, and
(2) Create ways to deal with the reasons that you smoked in the first place.

You will accomplish both these tasks so that when the day comes that you had planned to quit, you will be confident to do it.

HOW TO HANDLE THE URGE TO LIGHT UP

There are several choices that you can use in your fight to quit. EACH OF THESE CHOICES WORK- THEY HAVE BEEN PROVEN

You may use one, all, or a combination of several to achieve your goal. The urge to smoke is immediate, and usually lasts for five minutes. If you can resist for that period of time, you reduce the urge.

1. Take a deep breath, hold it for a few seconds, and exhale as if you had just taken your first puff on a cigarette. Part of the feeling you get from smoking is a direct result of taking a deep breath. A deep breath allows you to take in a maximum amount of oxygen, and exhaling lets out large quantities of carbon dioxide. This results in a feeling of relaxation. Try it, you'll see.

2. Take a sip of water several times during this five minute period. It can help to diminish the need to smoke, and gives you something to do with your hands. The extra water will also help to flush the nicotine out of your body.
3. Put something in your mouth that has no calories, such as a stirrer, toothpick, or another substitute for a cigarette.
4. Get busy with something, anything, to keep you busy for the next five minutes.
5. as long as it does not lead to a craving, chew a piece of gum or a piece of hard candy. Life Savers work well.
6. Get up and move around for five minutes. It will help the urge to smoke to pass.
7. Use a nicotine patch as replacement therapy. (It can lead to more cravings in some people).
8. Remember why you want to quit. Then say it out loud.

LET'S STOP RIGHT NOW!

The first thing to do is set a date when you are going to quit smoking. Let's start one week from today. That will give you plenty of time to practice with the choices in your list. Eight days from today, it will be the beginning of the end of your smoking habit.

Days 1 and 2

Examine your smoking behavior for the first two days. Every time you light up, ask yourself:

1. Why am I smoking this cigarette?
2. Would this be an easy one or a difficult one to do without?
4. If I did not smoke this cigarette, what would I do instead?

Day 3

Let's get out and test your strength today.

<u>At least once today, use your willpower to push down the urge to smoke.</u>

During the five minutes that it will take for the urge to pass, try out some of your choices. Try one, or all, or find a combination that works for you.

<u>Day 4</u>

Today is the big testing day. If you haven't already tried it, skip those one or two cigarettes that you feel may be the toughest to give up in your daily routine. Pick the ones that you rated "difficult" during your monitoring period.

Remember, this is a practice period, and you must not get upset if you are unable to give up a difficult cigarette. You must practice and experiment with your different choices to realize how you can be more effective.

If you found skipping that cigarette very difficult or even failed in the end, review any factor that got in the way of your success. The most common causes of difficulty or failure that a potential quitter faces are:

Chemical properties of addiction

When you do not have that cigarette, you feel lousy. If you are a heavy smoker, a nicotine patch may help to relieve your bad feelings.

Social pressures

You may find yourself in a situation (card game, party, coffee break) during which you would normally smoke. It may help to let others know of your desire to quit, and also your reasons for quitting. Enlisting the aid of a non smoker to confide in may also help. Make sure that he or she is aware of your goals so that they do not say or do anything to instill a negative impact on your desire to quit.

If you feel that you may not resist the social pressures of smoking, consider the option of giving up these social encounters for two or three weeks until the urge passes and you can be comfortable again.

Tension and negative emotion

A crisis occurs during your work or personal day, and one of the main reasons for you to smoke has been tension reduction. Try to deal with your negative emotions and use the tension reducing methods that we talked about earlier. Get away from the area that the tension is associated with. Take a walk, or go to another room. You may also find that nicotine gum will give you enough tension relief to get through.

Days 5, 6, and 7

You are now heading down the home stretch. In the next three days, your goal is to come out of this week smoking half the cigarettes that you would normally smoke. If you started as a one pack a day smoker, cut back to ten cigarettes per day, or less. The fewer the better. During days 5 and 6, set your goals toward achieving positive results on day 7. Maintain your smoking record during these three days, and continue to decrease your dependency on nicotine. What do you do if you still have doubts? This is probably due to your chemical dependency on nicotine. It is a highly powerful drug, and many factors have been working together to make you dependent. Discuss with your doctor about the feasibility of a patch or nicotine gum. Nicotine is the hook that has gotten you to smoke which carries the harmful effects to your body. With the help from the patch or the gum, you will have all he tools you need to successfully quit. The patch or gum will give you a steady influx of nicotine into your system, which will be reduced slowly over a period of several weeks. DO NOT SMOKE WHILE ON THE

PATCH. You could experience a dangerous overdose of nicotine.

NOTE; Pregnant women should not use the gum or patch, and should not be smoking at all. Smokers with any form of heart disease should consult with a physician before using.

DEALING WITH THE SYMPTOMS OF WITHDRAWAL

Dizziness may occur during the first one or two days. Take a quick break, it will pass.

Headaches may appear at any time during the first weeks. Try to relax. Take any usual remedy for headache, a cold cloth on the back of your neck, or relieve the stress by taking a short walk.

Tiredness may occur during the first few weeks, but if you meditate or relax during the first few weeks, it will pass.

Coughing may actually increase during the first few days, simply because the residue from the smoke

has not been flushed from your system.
Tightness in the chest may occur in the first few days. Rest and take deep breaths, it will go away.
Sleeping problems may occur in the first few days. Try to stay away from drinks that have a caffeine content, try not to exercise too strenuously in the hours prior to bedtime. A hot bath prior to retiring at night may also be helpful. Lavender essential oil between the toes also helps at bedtime and is calming.
Constipation may occur in the first month after you quit. If this occurs, eat foods with a high fiber content, drink plenty of fluids, and do some light exercise.
Concentration may tend to wander during the first few weeks. Be ready for this, take a break, or do something physical for a short period of time.
The following pages will give you an example form to chart your progress as you begin to give up

cigarettes. They are all self explanatory and should prove to be a tremendous asset in assisting you to give up your habit. On a daily basis, chart each cigarette that you smoke during the day.

Enter the time, place, and with whom you smoked, the reason for smoking, whether it will be easy or difficult to give that one up, and the weapon that you will use to fight the urge to smoke that one.

CONCLUSION

If you are not completely confident that you can resist the urge to smoke after you have quit, it may be necessary to remove any visual reminders of smoking from your living and work areas. Throw away or give away those leftover cigarettes, get rid of lighters, ashtrays, matches, and anything else that could be associated with smoking. Why should you force yourself to resist the urge to smoke when it is far simpler to just remove the reminders. If you keep a pack of cigarettes in your home or office, there is a good chance that you may pick one up. Just this one may be the cigarette that hooks you again.

CHARTS TO HELP YOU

DAY 1 - CIGARETTES SMOKED
DATE:

NO.	TIME	Place & With Whom	Reason for Smoking	E or D	CHOICE to Use
			1		
			2		
			3		
			4		
			5		
			6		
			7		
			8		
			9		
			10		

11
12
13
14
15
16
17
18
19
20
21
22
23
24
25
26
27
28
29
30
31
32
33
34
35
36
37
38

39
40

DAY2-CIGARETTES SMOKED
DATE:

NO.	TIME	Place & With Whom	Reason for Smoking	E or D	CHOICE to Use

1
2
3
4
5
6
7
8
9
10
11
12
13
14
15
16
17
18
19

20
21
22
23
24
25
26
27
28
29
30
31
32
33
34
35
36
37
38
39
40

DAY 3-CIGARETTES SMOKED
DATE

NO.	TIME	Place & With Whom	Reason for Smoking	E or D	CHOICE to Use

29
30
31
32
33
34
35

CIGARETTES ELIMINATED

NO. TIME Place & With Whom CHOICE Used E or D Comments

1
2
3
4
5

DAY 4-CIGARETTES SMOKED

DATE:

NO. TIME Place & With Whom Reason for Smoking E or D CHOICE to Use

1
2
3
4

5
6
7
8
9
10
11
12
13
14
15
16
17
18
19
20
21
22
23
24
25
26
27
28
29
30
31
32

CIGARETTES ELIMINATED

NO.	TIME	Place & With Whom	CHOICE Used	E or D	Comments
1					
2					
3					
4					
5					
6					
7					
8					

DAY 5-CIGARETTES SMOKED

DATE:

NO.	TIME	Place & With Whom	Reason for Smoking	E or D	CHOICE to Use
1					
2					
3					
4					

CIGARETTES ELIMINATED

NO.	TIME	Place & With Whom	CHOICE Used	E or D	Comments
					1
					2
					3
					4
					5
					6
					7
					8
					9
					10

DAY 6-CIGARETTES SMOKED

DATE:

NO.	TIME	Place & With Whom	Reason for Smoking	E or D	CHOICE to Use
			1		
			2		

3
4
5
6
7
8
9
10
11
12
13
14
15
16
17
18
19
20
21
22
23
24
25

CIGARETTES ELIMINATED

NO.	TIME	Place & With	CHOICE Used	E or D	Comments

Whom

1
2
3
4
5
6
7
8
9
10
11
12
13
14
15

DAY 7- CIGARETTES SMOKED

DATE:

NO.	TIME	Place & With Whom	Reason for Smoking	E or D	CHOICE to Use

1
2
3
4
5

6
7
8
9
10
11
12
13
14
15
16
17
18
19
20

CIGARETTES ELIMINATED

NO.	TIME	Place & With Whom	CHOICE Used	E or D	Comments
1					
2					
3					
4					
5					
6					
7					

8
9
10
11
12
13
14
15
16
17
18
19
20

HOMEOPATHIC TREATMENT OF SMOKING ADDICTION

A PROTOCOL GUIDE AND RESEARCH STUDY

(Desensitization of Cigarette Cravings

With Complex Homeopathy)

Abstract:

This is a paper on using a graduated desensitization program to help a group of twenty-three smokers become free from nicotine and tobacco dependency. They were tested for nicotine dependency. Successful treatment resulted in over twenty of the cases, showing both short- and long-term results in dealing with smoking addiction. Complex homeopathy is shown to be a possible treatment for stopping cigarette addiction.

Key Homeopathics to use:

Nicotine, smoking, addiction, Vitamin C, Anti-Smoking I, Anti-Smoking II, Lung Liquescence, Hygly; Heart, Lung homeopathic, endorphins, Endorphin homeopathic, Crystallized Cell Salts, Substance Abuse

Introduction:

Cigarette smoking and other types of nicotine usage have been with us for many years. The use of the natural herb known as tobacco as a stimulant has been extreme, and has complicated the health of many people. In fact, recent evidence shows that over seven hundred fifty thousand deaths a year occur in the United States as a result of smoking. World-wide estimates of smoking deaths well exceed the multi-millions per year because of this habit. Dramatic evidence now shows conclusively that smoking is a dramatic health risk.

Nicotine is a highly addictive substance. Manufacturers and retailers of these tobacco products try to ignore the fact that they are making accessible a highly addictive substance that can have dramatically detrimental effects on health. This type of substance abuse requires a complete reconsideration of the process of how and why we let such companies sell such a dramatically harmful product.

For the homeopath or naturopath a safe, natural process of bringing patients off cigarette addiction is very important. To this end it has been developed into a series of complex homeopathic treatments that can help the patient in this fight against addiction.

There is a two-step desensitization program for this. One has a concentrated amount of nicotine and the other has no nicotine whatsoever. The homeopath can help the patient in a graduated-step process to quit smoking. Most carcinogenic activity is from the burning of the paper and the various tars and carcinogens that are emitted by the flame

Intestinal or skin absorption of nicotine is less harmful than smoking, but is still harmful. For the patient who wants to quit and needs help, there are many substances available. Some use nicotine gum or patches for short-term treatment. Some just stop overnight.

For homeopathic treatment there is Anti-Smoking I, a homeopathic containing a low-potency (3x) of nicotine taken from tobacco and lobelia (Indian tobacco). This blend of ingredients, along with nux vomica and other classical homeopathics that are used to desensitize cravings is given to the patient to use when he feels the urge for a cigarette.

When a smoker wakes up in the morning, he usually wants to refurbish his blood nicotine levels by having a cigarette. He is to take ten to fifteen drops of the Anti-Smoking I formula under the tongue. Since sublingual and stomach absorption of nicotine is slower than respiratory absorption, the smoker must wait fifteen to twenty minutes for effects to set in. If by then he is still craving a cigarette, he may take a second dose. After another fifteen to twenty minutes of craving he may take a third dose. *He is not to take over three doses.* This generates a slight dose of nicotine into the blood to reduce craving. The time involved (twenty minutes) helps to reduce the craving as well, and also helps to stimulate endorphins.

People must realize that in any case of substance abuse or addiction involvement, if someone exhibits a behavior that gives him or her positive feelings (even through a drug); we must find *another* positive feeling to take its place. If we fail to do so, depression can ensue, which can push the person towards relapse. To get a good, healthy type of stimulus, we might have the patient resort to an exercise program such as jogging or swimming; or possibly a social program such as a network of friends. Perhaps a hobby would be useful for the patient to direct his activity; from this he can get a positive stroke, rather than seeking it from smoking.

The Anti-Smoking I formula is carried by the patient and used when needed during the first week or two of detoxification.

Ridding the blood of higher nicotine levels takes three to ten days. By prescribing the Anti-Smoking I formula we are shifting him from one source of nicotine to another. But the nicotine in the Anti-Smoking I formula is dramatically less than the amount absorbed by respiratory absorption of cigarette smoke. Thus patients will still deal with cravings at that point.

Nicotine is water-soluble. Thus every time a patient rids the body of water by urinating, heavy sweating or other ways, they will/may crave a cigarette. This is why a cigarette is craved after sex, a hot bath, eating or urinating. If the patient does not smoke (during the first week) for fifteen minutes before urination and an hour and a half after urination, then he is dealing with his nicotine craving at the most intense times.

Other methods can be used to help the smoker in the initial stages of smoking reduction. Creative visualization and mental control are very important in helping the patient to relax his mind, and decrease his urge to smoke. The point of any type of mental exercise is not to tell the patient not to smoke, as the mention of the word "smoke" puts the image in his mind, and makes him crave it even more. The patient should try to substitute a mental activity *for* smoking. He may meditate on a game or something else that would occupy his mind.

The major vitamins depleted by smoking are vitamins A, C and E. These vitamins must be supplemented into the diet to help rebuild the tissue and decrease the craving.

Vitamin A should be prescribed at 20,000 IFS a day, vitamin C at 1,000 - 3,000 mg a day, and vitamin E at 1,000 IFS a day. Extra vitamin C can also be given, as it is a strong stimulator of endorphins that help reduce the craving. Patients can also be taught to wrap a rubber band around the wrist, and upon craving snap the rubber band on the skin. This accomplishes several things: the pain stimulates endorphins and helps to stop the craving, and the craving is associated with the snapping rubber band, thereby desensitizing the patient through negative conditioning.

After the patient has taken Anti-Smoking I drops orally for a week or two, they may shift to skin application by putting three drops on the skin over an acupuncture point, such as those between the thumb and index finger (the hoku point), and the webbed area closer to the index finger. By massaging this into both spots, slight amounts of nicotine can be put into the skin, which also helps the patient by stimulating the acupuncture point. This acupuncture point is connected to many places in the body, and helps to correct blood sugar imbalance.

The hypoglycemia formula known as Hygly can also be used, as in any addiction, dealing with blood sugar oscillations is very important. The Substance Abuse homeopathic should also be used; this helps the body to correct for any substance abuse. Chromium is best for cravings.

After using the Anti-Smoking I formula, the patient may be directed to the Anti-Smoking II formula. None of the actual chemistry of nicotine exists in this formula, but the high potencies (over 30x) help to desensitize the energetic need. Anti-Smoking II is thus a safe formula that can be taken for long periods of time to help the patient to diminish craving and cleanse the body.

After a month of therapy with Anti-Smoking II, the formula may be put on the shelf and used only when the patient needs it to prevent or deal with relapse. It is very important that we caution the smoker about relapse and prepare him for its possible occurrence. Most smokers say that relapses seem to occur at ninety-day intervals; they go into places and see people smoking and relaxing. In their minds they see themselves relaxing that way, too. They don't realize at that point that nicotine relaxes by satisfying an internal addiction. The first time anyone has a cigarette (or someone has a cigarette after months), the cigarette can be rather disturbing to the system. That's because it is a noxious agent. Often a former smoker will have a cigarette or two, and resign himself to being a smoker again. This must be stopped if it occurs; the smoker must realize that he can still regain control and get back to not smoking. The Anti-Smoking II formula can help with that type of relapse.

Lung Liquescence and Heart, Lung homeopathic glandular are also helpful in rebuilding tissue and diminishing craving. The Endorphin homeopathic helps in diminishing craving too.

One side effect of quitting smoking can be an initial weight gain. It has been shown that weight gain can be avoided by taking 1,000 mg of coral calcium a day. The best formula we have for this is the Crystallized Cell Salts, which supplies a well-balanced blend of all needed minerals. Two tablets of cell salt formula a day supplies the need that helps prevent weight gain.

We can see that we also must emphasize behavioral factors such as exercise, proper motivation, will power, mind control, and healthy life style to deal with the cigarette craving. Sometimes desensitization programs must be resorted to, such as having the patient smoke a hand-rolled cigarette of coltsfoot herb. This herb rolled into a cigarette and smoked by the patient diminishes the patient's craving by taking away his taste for tobacco.

This type of desensitization works for other people. An associate of mine said that he had smoked when he went into the marines, and couldn't stop smoking. He snuck a cigarette one day, and the sergeant caught him. To desensitize him the sergeant had him smoke ten cigarettes rolled into one, and put a blanket over his head. The extreme concentration of tobacco made him violently ill, so that now he can't even think about touching a cigarette any more. This extreme desensitization sometimes is resorted to in extreme cases.

Methods:

For the purposes of the study twenty three cases were chosen who desired to quit smoking. After treatment they would get a follow-up call to determine how well they did at the end of every six-month period, up to a two-year period.

At the end of the first six-month period, all twenty-three were still not smoking. At the end of the first year, five had returned to smoking. They then used Anti-Smoking I and, after a year, quit smoking again. At the end of eighteen months a total of eight had returned to smoking, leaving fifteen who continued not to smoke after the initial program. Of these eight, three had withdrawn from the entire course of the study. Five had returned to smoking.

Discussion:

Many of the subjects said that the Anti-Smoking II was a big help; keeping it on their shelves helped them to get through relapses (noting that relapses seemed to occur in ninety-day cycles).

At the end of the second year only eight had started smoking again, and thirteen continued not to smoke. Two were not available to question. Three of the women had quit, but had returned to smoking (patients #7, #13, and #23). Three patients (#10, #17, and #20) also returned to smoking after six months. Thus the study was able to show that the program was successful. Motivation from their therapists, family, and friends was a primary factor in their success. Smoking becomes less and less desirable to society, as more people want to break the habit.

We can see from this study that most involved were helped by the graduated desensitization program. The program helped them to shift from inhalant nicotine to an oral source, and then after some time, a total high-potency homeopathic that would have no dangerous chemical compounds. This homeopathic helped to reduce the urge to smoke. The blend of nutritional factors, counseling, and motivation also were important in the success of this study.

HOMEOPATHIC TREATMENT OF SMOKING ADDICTION

A PROTOCOL GUIDE AND RESEARCH STUDY

(Desensitization of Cigarette Cravings

With Complex Homeopathy)

--- *BIBLIOGRAPHY* ---

1. **Essential Medicine.** Edited by Ried Jones. *Churchill Livingston,* 1993.

2. **Pharmacognosy** (9th ed.). Tyler, Brady & Robbers. *Lea Febiger,* 1988.

3. **Medical Botany.** Lewis. *Wiley,* 1977.

4. **Merck Manual** (15th ed.). Edited by Berkow, M.D. *Merck, Sharp and Dome Research Laboratories,* 1987.

5. **Pathophysiology: The Biological Principle of Disease.** Smith and Thier. *Saunders,* 1981.

6. **American Medical Association Home Medical Advisor.** Edited by Clayman, Kunz and Meyer. *Random House,* 1988.

7. **Differential Diagnosis**. Harvey and Bordley. *Saunders,* 1976.

8. **Statistics Manual.** Research Dept. US Naval Ordinance Test Station. *Dover, N.Y.,* 1960.

9. **The Essentials of Clinical Biochemistry**. D. N. Barron. *Elsevier Biomedical, Amsterdam*, 1982.

10. **Gray's Anatomy**. Henry Gray, Royal College of Surgeons. *Running Press, Philadelphia*. 1974.

11. **Homeopathic Pharmacopeia of the United States**. *Homeopathic Pharmacopeia Convention of the United States, Washington, D.C.* June 1993.

12. **Physician's Desk Reference** (3rd Ed.). *Medical Economic Data, Inc.* Montvale, N.J. 1992.

HYPNOTHERAPY

Many people use hypnotherapy to aid their quit smoking protocol.

When you are hypnotized it feels like being half awake and half asleep. You know where you are and your surroundings. It is not like TV hypnosis - you are always in control.

The hypnotherapist takes you to a deep state of relaxation by talking to you. You are usually sitting comfortably on a chair or recliner.

Follow ups may be needed but a CD is usually given to embed the hypnosis into the psyche.

It is extremely successful and to be recommended.

CIGARETTE BRAND	TYPE	TAR	NICOTINE
CARTIER Vendome	Filter	8 mg	0.8 mg
CARTIER Vendome Menthol	Filter	8 mg	0.8 mg
COURTLEIGH 120 Slims	Filter	14 mg	1.4 mg
COURTLEIGH	Filter	14 mg	1.3 mg
DUNHILL International	Filter	15 mg	1.4 mg
DUNHILL Menthol Mild	Filter	10 mg	0.9 mg
DUNHILL King Size Lights	Filter	9 mg	0.8 mg
DUNHILL Infinate Lights	Filter	9 mg	0.8 mg
DUNHILL Ultra Lights	Filter	5 mg	0.5 mg
DUNHILL King Size	Filter	15 mg	1.4 mg
MATRIX Lights	Filter	10 mg	1.8 mg
BENSON & HEDGES Gold	Filter	15 mg	1.4 mg
BENSON & HEDGES Special Mild	Filter	10 mg	1.0 mg
BENSON & HEDGES Ultra Mild	Filter	6 mg	0.6 mg
BENSON & HEDGES Menthol Mild	Filter	10 mg	1.0 mg
BENSON & HEDGES Ultimate Light	Filter	4 mg	0.4 mg
BENSON & HEDGES No.1	Filter	1 mg	0.1 mg
CAMEL	Filter	15 mg	1.1 mg

CAMEL Light	Filter	8 mg	0.7 mg
CAMEL Mild	Filter	13 mg	1.0 mg
CAMEL	Non-Filter	18 mg	1.4 mg
JOHN PLAYERS King Size	Filter	15 mg	1.0 mg
GAULOISES	Filter	12 mg	0.7 mg
GAULOISES Blondes	Filter	15 mg	1.1 mg
GAULOISES Legres Grey	Filter	9 mg	0.4 mg
GAULOISES Legres Red	Filter	5 mg	0.8 mg
GITANES	Filter	12 mg	0.7 mg
LUCKY STRIKE	Filter	12 mg	0.9 mg
LUCKY STRIKE Lights	Filter	9 mg	0.7 mg
CHESTERFIELD	Filter	13 mg	1.0 mg
CHESTERFIELD Lights	Filter	9 mg	0.7 mg
CHESTERFIELD	Non-Filter	17 mg	1.5 mg
CONSULATE	Filter	16 mg	1.3 mg
SATIN LEAF	Filter	11 mg	1.0 mg
SATIN LEAF Ultra	Filter	5 mg	0.5 mg
SATIN LEAF Ultra 1 mg	Filter	1 mg	0.1 mg

SATIN LEAF Ultra Menthol	Filter	5 mg	0.5 mg
SATIN LEAF Absolute Lights	Filter	3 mg	0.3 mg
CRAVEN A 120 Menthol	Filter	15 mg	1.3 mg
CRAVEN A	Filter	15 mg	1.3 mg
GUNSTON	Filter	17 mg	1.5 mg
JOHN ROLFE King Size	Filter	14 mg	1.2 mg
JOHN ROLFE Lights	Filter	7 mg	0.7 mg
LEXINGTON	Filter	17 mg	1.4 mg
LEXINGTON Lights	Filter	12 mg	1.1 mg
MILLS	Filter	17 mg	1.5 mg
PALL MALL	Filter	12 mg	1.1 mg
PALL MALL Super Lights	Filter	6 mg	0.6 mg
PETER STUYVESANT	Filter	15 mg	1.4 mg
PETER STUYVESANT Extra Mild	Filter	9 mg	0.8 mg
ROTHMANS King Size	Filter	15 mg	1.4 mg
ROTHMANS King Size Special Mild	Filter	12 mg	1.1 mg
VOGUE Slims 100	Filter	5 mg	0.5 mg
VOGUE	Filter	10 mg	1.1 mg
WINFIELD	Filter	14 mg	1.2 mg

WINFIELD Lights	Filter	10 mg	1.1 mg
WINSTON	Filter	15 mg	1.3 mg
WINSTON Lights	Filter	8 mg	0.7 mg
FORUM Mild	Filter	9 mg	0.6 mg
FORUM Estate	Filter	14 mg	1.0 mg
FORUM Menthol	Filter	13 mg	0.7 mg
EMBASSY King Size	Filter	15 mg	1.5 mg
EMBASSY Lights	Filter	11 mg	1.0 mg
EMBASSY Menthol	Filter	15 mg	1.5 mg
ROYALS Red	Filter	15 mg	1.4 mg
ROYALS Light	Filter	11 mg	1.0 mg
ROYALS Menthol	Filter	13 mg	0.7 mg
RIVAS PARK	Filter	15 mg	1.2 mg
SHARP	Filter	14 mg	1.2 mg
KINGSTON King Size	Filter	11 mg	1.0 mg

www.ingramcontent.com/pod-product-compliance
Lightning Source LLC
Chambersburg PA
CBHW070322290526
45791CB00003B/1214